HURT. HEAL. GROWTH

THE MEN'S BREAKUP DAIRY

PALLE VASU

Copyright © Palle vasu
All Rights Reserved.

This book has been self-published with all reasonable efforts taken to make the material error-free by the author. No part of this book shall be used, reproduced in any manner whatsoever without written permission from the author, except in the case of brief quotations embodied in critical articles and reviews.

The Author of this book is solely responsible and liable for its content including but not limited to the views, representations, descriptions, statements, information, opinions and references ["Content"]. The Content of this book shall not constitute or be construed or deemed to reflect the opinion or expression of the Publisher or Editor. Neither the Publisher nor Editor endorse or approve the Content of this book or guarantee the reliability, accuracy or completeness of the Content published herein and do not make any representations or warranties of any kind, express or implied, including but not limited to the implied warranties of merchantability, fitness for a particular purpose. The Publisher and Editor shall not be liable whatsoever for any errors, omissions, whether such errors or omissions result from negligence, accident, or any other cause or claims for loss or damages of any kind, including without limitation, indirect or consequential loss or damage arising out of use, inability to use, or about the reliability, accuracy or sufficiency of the information contained in this book.

Made with ♥ on the Notion Press Platform
www.notionpress.com

Contents

Preface — v

Acknowledgements — vii

1. BREAKUP DAIRY {HURT} — 1

HEAL & GROWTH

2. DENIAL — 45

3. PAIN AND GRIEF — 48

4. ANGER AND RESENTMENT & BARGAINING — 52

5. ACCEPTANCE {HEAL} — 55

6. SELF {GROWTH} — 59

7. THE ENTIRE STORY — 76

8. HOW TO BE SELF SATISFIED — 84

DOES RELATIONSHIP MATTERS? — 91

ABOUT THE AUTHOR — 97

Preface

This book is for the people who are unabe to move on or those who stay stuck, replaying memories of someone who no longer willing to stay. Through my own situations and lessons, I've written this as a guide, to the people who are culess after their heartbreak—Showing there's a way through it. If you're still holding on to someone who's gone, I hope these pages help you heal better

This book is written from my personal experiences—along with insights from research papers on dopamine and mental health. I've also included meaningful quotes from different books and from the Bhagavad Gita. To make sure my thoughts were accurate, I even took guidance from ChatGPT. After reading the early drafts, many of my friends encouraged me to publish it.

Take this book as a guide, not as a rigid research paper. Everything here is aligned with facts and reality.

ACKNOWLEDGEMENTS

To everyone who has experienced the heartache and uncertainty that a breakup can bring—you're not alone. You have more strength than you know: the strength to endure it, to hold it, to move through it. This book is for you; a tribute to the fortitude of the human heart!

I

BREAKUP DAIRY {HURT}

POST PHASE

<u>**OCT-2024**</u>

I gave you flowers, though they meant nothing to you,
I gave you affection, though it was never felt,
I gave you my time, but it never mattered,
I gave you myself, but you never cared.
The day I stayed silent, struggling to express my love,
The night I couldn't sleep, your messages echoing in my
mind,
My day ruined by the sting of your attitude,
My life shattered, knowing you deserve someone better.

<u>NOV 22 -2024</u>

ॐ

I packed my bags, escaping to Munnar,
But the memory of our argument lingered, unfinished.
I kept texting you, trying to fix what was broken,
Loving you even when you hated me the most.

—. TO BE CONTINUED

<u>ON A DAY NIGHT OCT- 2024</u>

ℬ

I've done everything I could... cried until my eyes hurt, wrote words I never thought I'd share, and still felt like pieces of me were slipping away—just to make you see how much you matter to me.

Yes, I care for you as a friend. But tell me—how do you stay just friends when your heart doesn't listen?

I admire you more than I can explain. You're in my head all the time, even in the smallest things. Every day, I tried—tried to bring you joy, to hear your laugh, to give you my full self. And yet, from you... it was often just a "hi," a "had dinner," a "good night."

But then there were those rare nights—we'd talk for hours, ten hours even. And those hours? They weren't just conversations. They were everything to me.

<u>A NIGHT IN NOVEMBER 2024</u>

જી

"Rika."
That's what I called you. A mix of logic and fragrance—because to me, you were both sharp and graceful. Strong. Brilliant. Beautiful.
But with that came your fire too... the anger, the resentment, the way your words sometimes cut through me like they were meant to leave scars.
And now, I see you with your friends—the ones who make you laugh, who fill your days, who give you everything I couldn't. Still... even with all of them around you, I can't shake off this thread that ties me to you. Something in me refuses to let go.

<u>ONE YEAR BACK</u>
<u>OCT-2023</u>

ༀ

Meeting you wasn't a coincidence,
It felt like fate, like I already knew you,
As if I'd carried you in my heart all along,
Caring deeply, loving quietly.
Choosing you was never easy,
A friend from afar, unseen, unheard—
Ten years of a silent journey,
Now beginning anew, as friends.

<u>NOVEMBER 2023</u>

৪৩

It wasn't easy to stop texting you,
Or waiting for your reply on that first day,
When you saw me only as a friend.
The silence was hard, but I let it stay.
It's not easy to quiet the anxiety,
To stop myself after such a long wait,
But I chose silence, chose humility,
And carried my love with quiet grace.

<u>DECEMBER 2023</u>

৪৩

The moments freeze in silence as you go offline,
I know I can't stop texting you,
Though I've paused for so many days.
I've sent countless snaps,
As anxiety grew,
Trying to speak to you as if I've waited years.
I know I can't make things unfold my way,
So I surrender,
Letting God decide what will be

YEAR LATER
OCTOBER 2024

You made me laugh with the first dialogue yeah i'm a goddess, but you made me cry with the last word of yours; you don't deserve me as a friend, yeah i dont deserve for being a just friend with you i need even more , i need to care even more., i need to hold you even more, i need to protect you even more, I need to love you even more

<u>YEAR LATER</u>
<u>OCTOBER 2024</u>

I waited for you through all those months while you focused on your exams. I was there for you during your breaks, supporting you every single time, never once imagining that my care, my possessiveness, would push you away. I'm the one who would stand by you when the whole world turns against you, the one who would be there to give you a place to feel free from every burden and responsibility.

YEAR LATER
<u>JANUARY 2024</u>

જી

My overthinking rises like a storm in heaven,
As the days slip by, I struggle to make things right.
Then a text appears, bringing joy I never expected.
I wasn't the same before,
I wasn't the one making my own way,
I wasn't the one who felt unlovable.
I know I lost my self-respect,
Talking to you as a friend,
But I can't be ghosted anymore.

YEAR BEFORE
JANUARY 2024

ॐ

Finally, you're back.
But no text. Not even a word to say you'd returned.
I was waiting—every second, every minute, every hour,
every day, every week. Waiting like a fool.
And then I asked, "Are your exams over?"
You just said, yes.
Casual. Cold. Like it meant nothing.
That's when everything hit me that how stupid I've been,
holding on, expecting more..
If I don't mean anything to you, then why even you
bothering replying?

<u>FEBRUARY 2024</u>

છા

Days feel rough as I wait for your messages, month after month.
Every moment apart makes me more anxious about reaching out to you.
Sometimes it's your attitude, sometimes it's your self-discipline—it all hits me hard,
knocking me down to a place I struggle to climb back from.
I know it's tough to just be friends with the girl I love most,
but I also know I can't let go.

<u>FEB 2024</u>

৪০

Do you remember the day we met?
Your eyes, like a cold shower.. froze me with every glance.
Your skin, the hue of dark chocolate, irresistibly drew me
in.
An innocent face, half-hidden behind a mask, only
deepened your mystery.
Your hair fell softly, framing eyes that told untold
stories—
Dark circles you laughingly called a sun tan.
You spoke to me for hours, your voice weaving a
connection I dared to hold on to.
And then, just as suddenly, you left.
With a parting smile, you blocked me—
A silent goodbye, yet loud enough to echo forever

<u>FEB 2024</u>

&

I started sending you requests on Snapchat, pleading with you so desperately that I felt I had lost all self respect. I begged for hours, holding to the hope that you'd give me a reason, an explanation.
Finally, you revealed the truth—that it was because you didn't like having male friends. I was the only one you had, and you wanted to remove me because I loved you.
Even then, even now, I couldn't stop loving you.

MARCH 2024

ಜ

Things got a little better when I stopped texting you every day.
When I pulled back... kept it to once in a while.
I used to message you all the time, waiting for your replies like they were answers I couldn't live without.
I told myself—focus on your career, celebrate her wins, be happy with the little things she shares.
And I tried. I really tried.
But the day you rejected me... something broke.
I started doubting myself.
Started feeling small.
Like I wasn't worth even your words.
Your cold replies—they cut deeper than I know how to explain.
Every one of them felt like I was standing there, waiting to be hit.
Now, every day, I'm fading into silence.
Trying to hold on to at least being your friend.
Wanting more but too scared to say it.
Too scared to ask you back.
Just... stuck.

<u>MARCH 2024</u>

ଞ

You started caring me, you started asking about my mental health you started asking myself, you started liking me you started texting me for hours, you started giving me importance in your life, you started caring, i felt i found my i found everything that i was been waiting for a decade, i found my true love thats you. And i lost the way i am, the way i used to focus on my works now im focusing you.

<u>March 2024</u>

৪৩

You gave me so many subtle signs,
Hints that love lingered between the lines.
I fell into a trap, so deep, so true,
Believing that love was shared by you.
Every day, I dreamed of us together,
Building a life that would last forever.
Your presence gave me courage anew,
To work harder, to reach further, all for you.
In that moment, I loved you so,
A love so deep, I couldn't let go.
I wanted to stay, to never part,
For you had a home within my heart.
You stood by my side, speaking so kind,
"I'm here as your friend, why do you mind?"
"Just go ahead, don't worry, I'll wait,"
Words that left me unsure of fate.
But now I see, those words were a chain,
Binding my heart to love's sweet pain.

<u>May 2024- Exam time as well</u>

ॐ

Your birthday was coming closer.
I'd been waiting for months—counting days, holding on
with this strange excitement.
I wanted to surprise you.
Something thoughtful. Something true.
Something that said, you matter to me more than you'll ever
know.
And even though I knew... deep down... you might not
even want it,
I still gave it anyway.
And for a moment—just a moment—you smiled.
You loved it. The air felt lighter.
It felt like we shared something real.
But then—your words.
Sharp. Cold. Out of nowhere.
"Delete my pictures."
And just like that, the joy was gone.
All I had left were the memories—
memories I can't erase, no matter how many times I try.

<u>June 2024</u>

As we used to text messages, I happened to see you in a group chat of your school, texting in a way that I lost completely. It triggered something within me, and I couldn't hold back—I confronted you.
You were openly fluttering with a guy whose face you didn't even know. You didn't seem like the person I once thought you were. The way you spoke to men was so different, so unlike the you I had envisioned.
I couldn't stay silent. I called you out, asking you to stop, to reconsider. And in the end, you listened.

JUNE 25

ॐ

We used to speak every single day,
Each moment bright, in its own way.
You drew me closer, I felt it too,
Treated me more than a boyfriend could do.
You saw me as someone important, rare,
Accepted my flaws, showed you care.
You embraced me just as I am,
A love so pure, no hidden sham.
I revealed my soul, my truest face,
A character others would often embrace.
You made me feel safe, at ease, at home,
Though anxiety whispered, "You'll end up alone."
I feared the loss, that ache, that sting,
But you brushed aside what my heart would bring.
You overlooked my actions, my love, my care,
Leaving me lost in the love we shared.
I scolded you today, it's true,
For words you spoke that didn't feel you.
Cringe they sounded, harsh they stayed,
I hated it, yet there I stayed.
You're always near, yet far from me,
So close to them, it's clear to see.
A side of you, now stark, revealed,
Different from the one I'd sealed.
I thought you innocent, kind, and sweet,
But chapri ways now seem complete.
With fluttering words, you play their game,
And yet, I stayed through hurt and shame.
You spoke with them, your tone so light,
A sting it left, deep through the night.

I wrote these lines, my feelings bare,
Hurt by a bond I thought we'd share.

<u>July 2024</u>

୫

We grew so close, it's hard to say,
Each passing May felt like a daydream's sway.
I'd picture trips, adventures untold,
And half-hugs where my heart felt bold.
I'd draw you near, to softly declare,
"I'm here to take over, to always care."
But tears would fall, my voice held tight,
As feelings hid in the quiet night.
When your love turned cold, began to stray,
I yearned to beg, "Please, just stay.
Stay with me, forever near,
Through joy, through sorrow, through every tear.

July half

&

I saw you start to share every little detail,
Opening up, letting your walls frail.
You trusted me, grew close, and stayed,
A love so pure, quietly displayed.
You cared for me in ways so kind,
Listening close, with an open mind.
You understood me, my flaws, my core,
And nurtured what we had, ever more.
Our situationship, you held with care,
Giving me hope, moments to spare.
Each day felt like a dreamy haze,
Talking to my crush, lost in the gaze.

August 2024

૭૩

You slowly began sharing about your Snapchat male friend,
How they proposed, and you'd still reply again.
Yet lately, you've started avoiding me,
Your distance growing, clear to see.
You mentioned one day, a strange request,
"Should I share my palm photo?"—you sought my best.
And when someone proposed, you left things vague,
Your short words gave hints, but truth seemed like a
plague.
I was triggered, asked, sought to know,
But you shared just fragments, your answers slow.
Each day I'd press, my curiosity grew,
Yet your silence deepened, ignoring me too

<u>AUG 2024</u>

ೞ

Slowly, the arguments began to rise,
Though I tried to stop, anger took its guise.
For two days, I was harsh, I admit,
Then things seemed fine, but you reopened it.
You mentioned another, hiding it well,
It made me question every truth you'd tell.
Each day I'd ask, the tension grew,
Until frustration took over you.
You started to avoid, turned your gaze,
Talking to him in countless ways.
Your late replies became my pain,
As thoughts of you with him drove me insane.
Yes, it's the truth, hard to endure,
But for me, each day was torture, unsure

<u>Aug 2024</u>

୫ଠ

One day, what I feared most finally came,
The words I dreaded, you said the same:
"We can't be friends; it's time to leave."
My world shattered, too much to believe.
The smile I knew began to fade,
Tears fell fast, my heart betrayed.
My chest grew heavy, anxiety soared,
An endless ache I couldn't ignore.
For ten long days, I begged, I cried,
Hoping to mend the divide inside.
But your response was cold, distant, unclear,
Treating me like a stranger near.
Yet through it all, I chose to stay,
Silent in love, though you pushed away.

<u>Sept 2024</u>

ॐ

Cold. That's what it felt like.
So cold it froze me where I was.
Phone in my hand, screen glowing,
and me—just sitting there, thinking,
why did I even pour my heart out if it meant nothing to you?
I'd been tossing in bed, restless,
when you pushed yourself into my mind again.
Not gentle—just sudden.
Like a reel of memories someone hit play on,
and I couldn't make it stop.
I sat up, chest tight, heart running ahead of me.
And then the tears came.
Not soft ones.
The messy, loud, embarrassing kind.
The kind you don't want anyone to see.
I didn't know what else to do.

<u>NOVEMBER 2024</u>

ॐ

*Panic attacks became a constant in my life, striking every
single night and creeping even into my morning. One
evening, a friend visited me and found me in a state he never
thought he'd see. Concern etched on his face, he said, "Let's go
on a trip. I think you need a break."
I could barely move, let alone think about leaving.
But somehow, I pulled myself together enough to throw
random clothes into a bag.
He went home, did the same.
And before I could process what was happening, we were
driving toward Munnar.
Not a planned trip. Not an adventure.
Just me running from my own head.*

<u>NOV 22 -2024</u>

ℬ

I packed my bags, escaping to Munnar,
But the memory of our argument lingered, unfinished.
I kept texting you, trying to fix what was broken,
Loving you even when you hated me the most.
I loved you in ways no one else could,
Cared for you while butterflies danced around,
But I chose you, and nothing ever mattered to you.
Each time I tried to make things right,
Your attitude triggered me,
Yet I silenced myself,
Not knowing how you drifted away,
Not understanding what changed you.
A decade of love,
Now lost,
Leaving me to drown in a thunderstorm of my own

<u>NOV - 2024</u>

∞

I begged, not once, not twice,
But countless times under silent skies.
You turned away, left my heart to ache,
How much more can a soul take?
You called me your best, your closest friend,
But your love seemed a signal you'd send.
We laughed, we loved, in moments so pure,
Now they're shadows—gone, obscure.
We texted like lovers, whispered like rain,
Dated like dreamers, free from pain.
Where are those words, those promises tight?
Do they vanish like stars swallowed by night?
You told me never to lose your trace,
Now I'm lost in this hollowed space.
Please, come back—hear my plea,
I'm dyeing here, can't you see?
Without you, life feels a cruel spell,
I've been trapped in my own personal hell.

In the golden hue of the morning, I've always wanted to pull you close, into my arms and impart to you a world of secrets and stories, a world of gossips and fables, built only for you.

I loved you with all my heart and wanted to tell you, you're never alone. You are a princess to me, and I am your faithful slave.

You were my happiness and the light during my darkest time. I wanted to be there, even in your worst.

I loved you like no one has ever, needed you like the sun needs the moon, and like a plant needs water.

I love you still, like no one will ever know, and still, I have cried a lot many of times, for you and for the fact that I never got to tell you.

So what's the final act of love?
Letting you go...

ॐ

How can I step away when I loved you above all?
How can I move forward when you were all I ever
dreamed?
How can I stop speaking to you when we once talked for
hours?
How can I leave it all behind when you are so special to
me?
How can I be myself when you are the one who brings me
joy?
How can I stop gazing into your eyes when they light up
my world?
How can I stop writing when you are the reason I found
my voice?
How can I stop dreaming when you feel like my reality?
How can I stop thinking when you're the one I cared for
the most?
How can I smile when the source of my happiness fades?
How can I let go when you're the reason I dared to chase
my dreams?
How do I say when everything falling
apart
How do I say when situations warped
around
How do I say when someone close had left
me
How do I say when it's.
hurting so badly
Is this a downfall? I was having Is this a new beginning Is
this what my fate is?

PALLE VASU

Is this what I wish for
Is this the end that I was expecting to be

> ""*What went wrong? Was I too much? Or maybe I wasn't enough? Why couldn't I just let go? Every moment replayed in my mind, like a never-ending loop, making the pain worse. I was drowning in questions, unable to breathe, unable to find peace.*""

"

Why can't I just let her go?
Is it because I still think maybe or just maybe there's a chance?
Or is it because I don't know how to face the space she left behind?
Why I'm I keep begging her to come back?
Everytime "no" feels heavier than the last.
What if this really is it? What if it's already over?
Should I just let go?
But what if tomorrow she wakes up and realizes she was wrong?
What if she actually needs me—and I've already walked away?
What if letting go becomes the biggest mistake of my life?
What if I wasn't so nervous all the time?
Would it have mattered? Or would I still be here drowning in these what ifs?
Why does my mind keep shouting—
you never got closure, you can't just leave it like this?
Am I begging her back for her?
Or just to calm the noise in me?
Why I have stuck in this loop?
Trying to change her mind, knowing she doesn't feel the same as mine
Why do I keep thinking love is something I can prove?

Around 3 in the morning, a cat wandered down the road, its eyes catching the faint light. It moved slow, sniffing, like it was hunting something, but stopped dead when it reached a patch of dark that seemed to swallow the street. A few crooked tombstones stood there, damp and mossy, the kind you avoid without thinking. The cat turned quick and slipped back toward the light.

A little further down was a house. Fresh paint, nets on the windows—it looked new at first glance. But up close, the cracks showed. The walls had stains, dust clung to the corners, and the silence inside felt heavy. Books were everywhere—open ones on the floor, piles slanting on chairs, dog-eared stacks on the bed.

On that bed, a man slept. He jerked awake suddenly, gasping like someone had pulled the air from his lungs. His chest burned. For a second he thought—this is it, this is a heart attack. He froze, couldn't even move. And then, as quick as it came, the pain slipped away, leaving him shaking.

He broke down. Not quiet tears—loud, choking sobs. His hands fumbled for his phone, desperate. Through the crying he muttered, "Come back... please, come back." The words cracked, falling apart into more sobs that echoed through the cluttered room.

ဆ

This is the poetric version of a story of a guy. He loved a girl so much that it ended up breaking him.

If I had to put his love into words, it was like the guy in the movie 96. He finally confessed, but she kept him as a friend. And you know how that feels—when your heart wants everything but all you get is "just a friend." I told him it would hurt more down the line, but like every one-sided lover, he convinced himself it was better than losing her completely. At least I can stay close to her for a while, he thought.

But she barely replied to his texts. When she did, her answers were short, sometimes so dry they cut him in ways he couldn't explain. She even made him feel cheap just for replying instantly, as if his care was something shameful. He tolerated it—for five months straight. Then, just when he thought things might change, she started getting closer to him. That's when he admitted, almost helplessly, I'm an overthinker.

And he was. He clung to her presence because he had already taken so much pain in her name. Then one day, he saw her talking to another guy—her tone, her pride, her distance. But even then, he refused to see her clearly. His insecurity spoke louder. Soon, she started avoiding him, because he was "too available." Even when she scolded him, humiliated him.. he stayed silent

Later, she began chatting with random guys on Snapchat. He saw the kind of people they were flirting with her. Insecure he told her that once, twice, three times. The fourth time, he asked her straight. She didn't argue. She blocked him. Everywhere.

He broke. He begged her to come back, tears flooding every word. She replied with nothing but attitude, as if he was already erased.

From there, it spiraled. His mind tortured him with questions: What if she's texting them and getting close? What if she's already forgotten me? Even if she forgive, he couldn't stop asking her about it, and that only pushed her further away. In the end, she blocked him off in every platform.

It left him empty. He loved her with everything, and all he got back was this unbearable sense that he wasn't enough. His confidence, his self-respect. Everything that once made him fight through life. Left with nothing but unbearable pain

At the same time, he was preparing for an entrance exam. That breakup hit so hard, he couldn't qualify. I've watched him since—seen the panic attacks with my own eyes.

I won't justify him, and I won't justify her either. He was drowning in depression. Overthinking became a part of him—it drained her too. He cried until nothing was left, but his anxiety grown higher. He was afraid of losing her, and in the end, that was exactly happened. He was good for her, but his mental illness twisted things until he judged her wrongly and had pushed her further away.

I just hope she's at peace, and I hope she understands that he was the not the one before, he never meant to hurt her.

This book is for people like him, for those who was not able move on, who stay stuck in the past, replaying memories of someone whose not there. Through my own sitation and lessons, I'm writing this as a guide. Not to dwell in pain, but to show there's a way through it. If you're holding on to someone who's gone, I hope these pages help you heal too.

I just hope she's at peace, he never meant to hurt her.

But that's only his side of the story. From where he stood, he gave her everything. From where she stood, maybe it felt different. Maybe to her, his love was heavy, even suffocating. Maybe she saw him as the one who made things harder—too intense, too serious, too old-school.

She was modern, more western in her way of thinking—lighthearted, playful. He was like a boy from the 90s—quiet, reserved, never the type to crack jokes or keep the mood easy. To him, that was normal. To her, maybe it wasn't enough.

So, while he calls it love, maybe she remembers it as something else. Maybe she remembers the weight of it more than the warmth.

HEAL & GROWTH

Here, it feels like you've lost your entire world—something everyone faces one day. The art of detaching from what you love the most is incredibly difficult, though not for everyone. But why isn't it hard for them? Why is it only hard for me? This question keeps pulling you down.

In a relationship, there are three types of people:

1. *The most caring– They see the other person as their entire world.*

2. *Moderately caring– They care but have many other priorities to focus on.*

3. *The indifferent – They don't care much, as they view relationships as a distraction from more important matters.*

4. *overthinking patner.*

Most of the time, the ones who care the most end up falling for the ones who hardly stays at all. It's cruel, isn't it? You pour your whole heart out, and they just... will not give it back. Not because they're evil or cold, but because something inside them just doesn't connect the same way.

See, the indifferent ones aren't heartless. They just have their priorities stacked differently. Work. Ambition. Survival. They put those above emotions, and for them, relationships are often second place. Sometimes it's their personality—they're more rational than emotional. Sometimes it's pain—has been hurt them before, so they build walls across them.

And yet, people get pulled to them. Why? Because they're a mystery. They don't reveal much. And that silence, that distance—it makes you want to dig deeper, to be the one who finally unlocks them. Especially if you're the caring type, you start hoping your love will be enough to melt their walls.

But here's the truth: it's exhausting. Loving someone indifferent feels like chasing a shadow. You give and give, waiting for a spark that never comes. And you're left asking yourself: Do they even care? Or are they simply afraid?

They're not emotionless. They just love differently, in a way that rarely matches what you expect. They call it strength—this detachment. But honestly? It's more like a barrier. It keeps them safe, but it also keeps them from ever really feeling close to anyone.

And about breakups... there's no magic trick. If you've been fully attached, letting go takes time. A lot of it. But trust me, it's worth it. Not in the dramatic "Arjun Reddy" way, drowning yourself in self-destruction. No, no. like Hardik Pandya—you take the fall, you struggles, and then one day, you come back stronger.

<u>OVERTHINKER</u>

Dating an overthinker is like stepping into a world where you have no escape—and even if you do, you'll always come back. They are a rare species of loyalty. They're not just green flags, they're green forests—choosing you even after a thousand arguments.

1. *They Analyze Everything You Say*

You text, "Hey, what's up?"
In their head: "Why just 'hey'? Are they bored of me? Is this the start of the end? Did I say something wrong? Maybe they're just tired. Or maybe they don't care. Should I even reply? Wait, if I don't reply, will they think I'm mad? Or desperate if I reply too soon?!"
And this is all before they actually type, "Not much, you?"

2. ***Overthinkers Plan the Future... Immediately***

After the second date, they're not thinking about where to grab dinner next time; they're wondering if your furniture will match theirs when you move in together. They've already pictured your wedding (and stressed over the guest list). Casual dating? For an overthinker, every coffee date comes with a side of "Are we soulmates?"

3. *Reading Signals is a Full-Time Job*

You laughed at their joke? Great, they're already imagining a comedy duo career for the both of you. You didn't respond to a meme they sent? They're drafting

an apology text for something they might have done
wrong.
With an overthinker, your every word, glance, and emoji
gets CSI-level scrutiny.

4. *They Care Deeply—Maybe Too Deeply*

While they're overthinking, one thing is clear: they care. A
lot. An overthinker will notice the tiniest things. You say
something in passing, and weeks later, they'll bring it up
like it mattered. They'll show up with your favorite snack
when you weren't even expecting it. You sneeze once, and
suddenly they're asking if you're okay, if you've taken
medicine, if you need water.

Dating an overthinker means you'll never wonder if they
care—they make it obvious. Sometimes too obvious. But
one thing's for sure: you'll never doubt their effort.

.

5. *Arguments Are... Exhausting*

Disagree with an overthinker, and prepare for a full
breakdown of every possible outcome of the fight.
Them: "Are we fighting? No? Okay. But what if we did?
Would we stop talking? Or would we make up
immediately? Wait, do you think I'm too confrontational?
Should I apologize just in case? But what if I'm over-
apologizing?"
You: "I just said I didn't want pineapple on the pizza..."

If you can handle their internal debates, you'll find that overthinkers are loyal, thoughtful, and deeply empathetic. They'll never forget your birthday, your pet's name, or that one time you casually mentioned liking green tea three months ago. They aren't for casual dating because they're wired to care too much—and honestly, that's what makes them special.

Dating an overthinker is a challenge, yes, but it's also a rewarding adventure. Just bring patience—and maybe a flowchart.

FACT

"Approximately 73 percent of the college students fall in love and dive in a relationship but less than 20 percent will become partners. Well what about the 53 percentages? Well everyone says its a god destiny, but can they hold onto their relationship? Because. infidelity, emotional distance, and lifestyle incompatibility. also external pressures, including family expectations, cultural constraints, and financial stress" MODERN DAY PROBLEM, ufff

II
DENIAL

The first day after a breakup would be the hardest part in your life. Suddenly, loneliness will hit harder in a way that you can't prepare . Half of you still waits, hoping they'll come back at any moment, and you're ready to accept them if they do. But the truth is, not every relationship runs on mutual effort. Most of the times, one person suffers while the other moves on as if nothing happened.

There's a dialogue in Arjun Reddy—or maybe it was Kabir Singh—that says, "Suffering is personal." And it's true. Nobody else can feel the pain way you do. You have to go through it on your own.

These days, it's easy to look for shortcuts like Tinder, Bumble, endless dating apps. Jump into something new just to escape from past. And yes, in the beganing it feels fresh and relief. But on a long run, it only deepens the wound. Healing will take time. Skipping it is like putting a bandage over a cut without cleaning it—it covers for a while, but the pain returns, sharper. Then there's alcohol. Many turn to it, thinking it'll numb the hurt. Drink after drink, trying to drown it out. But you don't escape. You just wake up with the same pain still holdig inside you.

So, what do we have to do? To detach ourselves from the pain and, more importantly, from the person who caused it?

෴

Let's see what bhagavad gita tells us
Dukhesv anudvigna-manah sukhesu vigata-sprhah;
vita-raga-bhaya-krodhah sthita-dhir munir ucyate"
(Chapter 2, Verse 56)

"A person who is not disturbed by distress and is not elated by happiness, and who is free from attachment, fear, and anger, is called a sage of steady mind."

This doesn't mean you have to ignore your feelings and act like nothing happened. Life is filled with ups and downs-- from the moments of joy to times of pain. A steady mind will never avoid these waves but learns to stay calm through them. You can do the same—not by pushing away your pain but by letting it teach you, which helps you grow stronger with each step forward.

Well to say most of us will prefer wine and breakup songs over all these some of us would walk through empty spaces to hide their pain well that's the biggest trap you do to yourself to dive into depression.

Stop avoiding the pain—accept it, feel it, and let it teach you. Stop seeking distractions in other things, and instead, realise you're strong enough to thrive on your own. Life may not sound as same as before, but this is your chance to rebuild yourself. If you want someone to love deeply, start with yourself.

So, Speaking about them is easy but how do we apply them?

Let me put it simply: Bro, no matter who you are or what type of situation you're facing, do you really think love is the only way to survive?

Whatever happened between you two—let it be. Don't go back and try to fix things on your own, Let them go. Move on. It's not as hard as it feels. Accept that they left you, or that things didn't work out, and focus on stronger growth.

Start traveling.

Traveling isn't as expensive as you think, but it understands you the real meaning of life. Don't stay locked up in your room, isolating yourself, Just as everyone does after their breakup. Get out there. Start discovering the world—and yourself.

Do the things that truly matter to you. If you loved reading novels, start doing it again. If singing brought you happiness, start singing. If playing a sport once your thing, get back to it. Do whatever makes you happy.

Think back at your childhood days—how were you then? And how are you now? Start reconnecting with that sense of joy and wonder you once had. Bring your happiness back. This is what personal growth is all about.

See, the only thing you're doing is replacing your past dopamine (her) with habits—the same dopamine your brain used to release when you talked to her—and that's what people call self-growth.

> ***"And yeah, one more thing—stop listening to Anuv Jain's Husn."***

III

PAIN AND GRIEF

It's really tough to handle. The pain and grief at the same time that come with loss-- hurts us unbearable, but they're also known for the first steps toward healing. That pain, as heavy as it shows how deep the bond really was and it reminds us that even in our darkest times, we can still find strength-- And we can still grow

This is the stage where everyone tends suffer, isn't the face we go through or a lot people goes through yet we desired to leave lash

Lets see how science say about breakup

1. **Neurochemical Responses**

Dopamine and Reward Systems: When you are in a romantic relationship, your brain automatically releases dopamine. is a neurotransmitter associated with pleasure and reward. This creates feelings of happiness and attachment. When suddenly the relationship ends, dopamine levels drop, which leads to a feelings of sadness and loss. These hormones are often referred as "**bonding hormones**" because they promote attachment and bonding between partners. the sudden drop in oxytocin and vasopressin—the hormones tied to bonding—can leave you feeling lonely and craving that connection again.. *In many cases, people who lived boring lives with no enjoyment or who feel lonely all the time, when they're in a relationship, will experience a high release of dopamine. Because the brain always craves for happiness; it doesn't want to stay stuck in boredom. So, when it finally receives dopamine through a relationship, it automatically absorbs even more deeply.*

A breakup does not only hurt your heart, but it will shakes the whole body. When we go through it, our brain releases cortisol—the stress hormone. And when cortisol rises, the body starts reacting. Your heart beats faster than average, headaches occurs without warning, nights turns into sleepless.

It doesn't stop with the body— But your emotions also twist. Anxiety creeps in, irritation increases over little things, and even the silence feels heavy. This is the reason-- why heartbreak feels so exhausting—it's not only sadness, but your entire system fighting the stress.

Experimental brain scan studies using functional magnetic resonance imaging (fMRI) tell us that the brain regions involved in emotional pain, heartbreak for example, are the same brain regions involved in physical pain. The anterior cingulate cortex and insula are involved in both types of pain. This is one reason why emotional pain can match the intensity of physical pain. The ventral tegmental area (VTA), the brain region involved in the reward circuitry, is also engaged when feeling romantic love. The VTA, in a post-breakup state, may shift from activity to one of diminished activation, which can lead to feelings of emptiness and depression.

Heartbreak is not just stories of feeling; it is literally the brain trying to reclaim the strongest source of positive reinforcement and reward which is simply YOU.

Every break up is felt as an abrupt event, a crash that leaves you crushed, battered and broken in places you never knew you could hurt. In the aftermath of the crash, you have an absence, an absence from which a sense of self has departed. No longer connected thinking becomes meta thinking, it spirals into chaos and confusion like leaves caught in a storm and the heart feels heavy with grief, burdened with the overload of it all.

But then there are the waves, unexpected and unrelenting and sometimes triggered by memory, a scent or a song that comes crashing down, an overwhelming tidal wave of sadness that functions almost as a flood. Breathing becomes a hard job, the heart is seized, bound in chains you cannot see, tears spill uninvited like rain, painfully as distinct from the chaos around you but it HURTS! It's as if nothing holds time and you are frozen in a moment of unbearable stillness and silence; you wish for relief but fear what that sight might hold.

Panic attacks, while very scary, can sometimes feel like your brain has decided to go rogue and hit the self-destruct button...for no reason! Your heart starts racing like you just completed a marathon (but the only thing you are doing is standing in line for coffee), your breath abandons ship, and your body behaves like you are being chased by a bear when it's really just Tuesday.

If ignored, panic attacks can spiral into avoiding places or situations where you have previously experienced panic attacks at. It's almost as though your brain is trying to transform you into a hermit to protect you and keep you "safe." The good news is they are manageable with the right help, and you can train your brain to stop being so overdramatic.

.

"दुःखेष्वनुद्विग्नमनाः सुखेषु विगतस्पृहः।
वीतरागभयक्रोधः स्थितधीर्मुनिरुच्यते॥"
(Bhagavad Gita 2.56)

Translation:

"One whose mind remains unshaken amidst sorrows, who does not hanker after pleasures, and who is free from attachment, fear, and anger, is called a sage of steady wisdom.

Let it be difficult to you, let it hurt, let it throw you off – let it do all of that and make you cry.. if that is how you feel. Even feel like it is breaking you. That is fine. But then, stop and ask yourself whether this breakup can really define you? What does it matter in the greater context of your lives? Like any human, your worth is not constant on another's love or rejection. So, at the end of the day.. it is you how well you can love yourself, regardless of what you have lost.

I knew that they meant everything to you, your entire world. But think about this—what about your parents watching you crumble like this? Is this what- they dreamed of seeing? Is this what you imagined for yourself when you were younger?

Get back up. Find your strength. Let it hurt for a while—it's okay to feel broken sometimes. But don't let it define you. Even a rough, unpolished rock has to endure pressure and forces to become a brilliant diamond. You will too.

"It will break you, for a better you"

IV

ANGER AND RESENTMENT & BARGAINING

Anger is also one of the first and strongest emotions after a breakup. It only comes from the pain, but also from the feeling of betrayal or unfairness. While anger is natural, it often works as the shield in protecting us from raw vulnerability and at the same time, it drains our energy and clouds our clarity.

From a psychological view, anger gives the illusion of control. It triggers the body to "fight or flight" mode, by releasing adrenaline and cortisol, which will create a brief sense of power. But carrying that state for too long becomes toxic. It traps us in a cycle where our own judgments are blurred, and we remain stuck to the past from where we want to move on .

And then comes resentment. Unlike anger, it's easy but no less harmful. Resentment lingers in the background, replaying old wounds again and again, always searching for reasons to justify the pain—while slowly corroding us from within.

∞

In The Bhagavad Gita, Chapter 16, Verse 21, Krishna warns:
"There are three gates leading to this hell—lust, anger, and greed. Renounce these, for they lead to the degradation of the soul."
This wisdom is a reminder that holding on to anger and resentment doesn't harm others as much as it harms us.

Bargaining comes next, subtly taking the place of anger. It is a phase of "what ifs" and "if onlys." You begin replaying scenarios in your mind: If I had said this differently... If I had been more understanding... If I could just make them see how much I care.

This stage is fueled by the human need for control. Bargaining is an attempt to reverse reality, to make sense of the chaos by believing you could still change the outcome. But life doesn't work that way.

∞

The Bhagavad Gita, Chapter 2, Verse 47, reminds us:
"You have a right to perform your duties, but not to the fruits of your actions."

This verse underlines the importance of effort over outcome. No amount of bargaining can undo what has already happened.

∞

<u>From literature, Khaled Hosseini's</u>
The Kite Runner provides a poignant example of the
futility of bargaining:
"There is a way to be good again," a character says, offering
hope for redemption. But redemption doesn't undo the past; it
requires facing it. Bargaining gives the illusion of change
without true acceptance.

Let go of everything—after all, we are human. Nobody does anything without their own psychological reasons or conditioning. For example, when we see a rapist, we belive them as harmful, but the actual truth is—they are humans too . Their actions weren't inherently monstrous; they were shaped by their situations and mindset.

Why am I telling you this?

Because at this stage, you might find yourself controlled by anger—not in the context of a crime like rape, but in the intensity of that same uncontrollable emotion. If you let this anger controls over you, it can lso cause immense suffering to the people around you. Learn to stay clam and composed. Be cold, even in situations like these. Even if she reaches you or tries to return to your life, respond with kindness and gentleness, but don't lose your balance.

The world is full of kind hearted people, if you
didn't find one

just be the one

V

ACCEPTANCE

{HEAL}

Acceptance isn't something that happens in a one go or a single moment but it's a gradual process. It doesn't arrive with celebration or a sense of winning. Instead, it comes slowly and quietly, while unnoticed, its like a soft shift inside you and that acts as a bandage. You feel it when the storm or the pain within starts to settle, when the coutless questions that you had begin to fade, and when you stop searching for answers in places that you will never be found. And thats how you find peace in the accepting fact that you no longer have to carry memories with you.

<u>The Psychology of Acceptance</u>

Psychologists are often describe acceptance as the final stage of grief. this is the point where denial, anger, bargaining, and sadness gradually make way to clarity. Our brain has an incredible ability to adapt. With the time those neural pathways that had lit up with pain begin to rewire themselves, making space for new experiences and fresh perspectives.

But acceptance isn't the same as being free of pain. It doesn't mean the hurt completely disappears but it means you've learned to acknowledge it without letting curse run your life. The past no longer feels like a wound you need to fix or a story you're forced to relive. Instead it will be in part of your jurney

Acceptance in the Bhagavad Gita

The Bhagavad Gita offers profound insights into the nature of acceptance. In Chapter 2, Verse 13, Krishna says: "Just as the soul continuously passes, in this body, from boyhood to youth to old age, the soul similarly passes into another body at death. A self-realized soul is not bewildered by such a change."

This verse reminds us that change is part of life and that the more we cling to what was, the more we suffer. Acceptance is not resignation it is realizing that life is constantly changing, and that every experience is simply a leg of our journey.

In Chapter 2, Verse 14, Krishna further explains:

"O son of Kunti, the nonpermanent appearance of happiness and distress, and their disappearance in due course, are like the appearance and disappearance of winter and summer seasons. They arise from sense perception and one must learn to tolerate them without being disturbed."

Acceptance means allowing the moments of your life to happen without judgment and knowing that those things happen because that's life!

From Literature and Life

In The Alchemist by Paulo Coelho, Santiago's journey teaches a profound lesson about acceptance: "When we strive to become better than we are, everything around us becomes better too."

Acceptance does not mean standing still, it is a movement towards persistence or growth. Acceptance is letting go of things that may not change, and putting your experience towards things you can change.

A principle echoed in the Serenity Prayer:

"Grant me the serenity to accept the things I cannot change, the courage to change the things I can, and the wisdom to know the difference."

How to Embrace Acceptance

Let Go of the Past: Get away from the idea of what could have been.. Focus on what is.

Practice Gratitude: Instead of being depressed on what you lost, appreciate what lies ahead.

Embrace yourself: Acceptance often comes in the silent moments of quiet reflection. Use this particular time to reconnect with yourself with the nature with meditation, with the things that helps you grow

Know Purpose: Turn this energy toward goals and passions that bring happiness and meaning to your life.

Trust the Journey: Life has a way of leading you to exactly where you need to be. Accept the faith that they no longer be with you.. In fact you'll find something better

Quotes to Reflect On

From The Bhagavad Gita:

"Detachment does not mean denying life. It simply means living without the constant fear of losing what you cherish."

"One who is self-controlled and unattached to the fruits of his work obtains peace and freedom from bondage." — Chapter 5, Verse 12

From literature:

3. "The moment you accept what troubles you've been given, the door will open." — Rumi

4. "Acceptance doesn't mean resignation; it means understanding that something is what it is and that there's got to be a way through it." — Michael J. Fox

Reflection

Acceptance is not an end of the past but it is a transformation of how you view it. It's the realization that every heartache, every panic attack, every tear, and every unanswered question that led you to this moment—a moment where you are stronger, wiser, and intelleual ready to move forward.

It is in acceptance that you are able reclaim your power, allowing the hurt to settle down and that no longer the tapestry of your life, no longer as a wound but as a thread of growth.

VI

SELF {GROWTH}

Growth and renewal are the gradual process after a breakup, through each stage of healing. It's not a straight path but a cycle of learning, unlearning, and becoming. Each stage offers lessons , opportunities for reflection, and a chance to emerge stronger.

1. Growth Through Denial: Finding the Courage to Face Reality

Breaking Through Denial

Denial is the first thing our mind throws at us after heartbreak. It works like a shield, by blocking some of the pain so we won't be crushed by all of it at once. In the short term, it actually help us to get a little breathing room in order to process unbearable pain. But the danger is, if you hold there too long, denial turns into a trap. It keeps you living in an illusion instead of facing reality. Real growth begins the moment you stop hiding from the truth. Its all about accepting and facing it with courage.

To heal, Is to face your feelings first. Let them come in. Don't dismiss them. Don't judge yourself for having them. Recognize what's there as sadness, anger, confusion, fire, whatever it is. Naming it is the first step in the healing process.

For some people, writing heals. Journaling will help to overcome, It can hold or even disappear the chaos in your head. When you put emotions into words, even messy ones then you start making sense of what you're going through. Sometimes just watching it on the page makes it feel lighter.

Talking it out helps too. Find someone you trust and let you share everything. A friend can be a sibling or anyone that won't judge you. Sharing the pain does not take the pain away but will lighten the burden you are carrying. And more often than not, the lens of another person will direct you to something you could not see alone.

It's important to remember this that denial isn't weakness. It's not failure either. It's just a phase of healing, a pause that gives you strength before you face the harder parts. But it's a stop, not the final destination. At some point, you have to move past it. And when you have, that's when real healing starts.

&

Denial will not last forever. The actual progress begins when you choose clarity over comfort.. Clarity allows you to see things clearly as truly they are, not as you wish them to be.

This shift from denial to clarity is where transformation begins. By accepting the reality, you reclaim your strength and open the door to growth. Clarity is not just an ending to denial but it's the beginning of a stronger, wiser you.

<u>Quote from the Bhagavad Gita:</u>

"Knowledge destroys the ignorance of the soul, like the sun dispels darkness." — Chapter 5, Verse 16

Acceptance of the truth is the first ray of light in your

journey of growth.
2. Growth Through Pain and Grief:
Embracing Pain as a Teacher

Pain is not merely an ailment, but it is a teacher. Pain makes you confront your shortcomings. Pain puts your vulnerabilities on display, it shines a spotlight on where you are wounded, and where healing must be served. Through lessons, grief cultivates such things like empathy, patience, and the ability to embrace the depth of life. Pain, while substantial, presents an opportunity for you to unveil your opportunity to appreciate your resilience, and to evolve.

The Process of Renewal

Self-Care:

Healing may not take place all at once. but in small, steady acts of kindness to yourself.

Allow yourself space to cry if the emotions keep rising. Tears are simply a release and not weakness.

Balance the serious moments with things that ground you or bring you peace. Some examples may be nature walks, reading a favorite book, or listening to calming music and even getting to razz one of your own friends.

Accept the Depth of Your Feelings:

Pain makes you to feel deeply. By allowing yourself to experience your emotions fully and then you give yourself permission to heal completely.

ॐ

Pain is a not a punishment or consequence; it is a pathway. If you stop holding onto it and start to see it as an opportunity, it changes from emotional burden to emotional strength.

Pain helps you discover parts of you didn't know where there; your strength, your patience, your empathy. It's in that realization you begin to reconstruct your self to be better than before.

Quote from Literature:

"Without pain, how could we know joy?" — John Green, The Fault in Our Stars

3. Growth Through Anger and Resentment:

Transforming Anger into Growth

Anger feels as powerful tool because it hides your vulnerability.. giving you a sense of control over your emotions. Since it's a natural response to pain, uncontrolled anger can become destructive, making you stuck in the past. Growth begins when you learn to work with this intense energy into something purposeful and constructive.

The Process of Renewal

Release Anger Physically:

Anger builds tension in the body. Making it into physical activities can provide relief and clarity over things.

Start running, yoga, or boxing to release pent-up frustration.

Try creative things like painting, writing, or playing music to transform your resentment into meaningful therapy.

Reflect and Reframe:

Take your time to understand the source of anger. Often, it's rooted in deeper pain or unmet needs. Acknowledge these feelings and seek ways to address them constructively.

The Key Shift

Holding onto anger keeps you triggered to the past, replaying the things that hurt you over and over. The true breakthrough comes when you start recognize that forgiveness, whether for others or for yourself is not about excusing the hurt but freeing yourself from its grip of struggling.

let go of anger, reclaim your energy and open the door to inner peace. Anger, when channeled wisely, can become a force of change, leading you toward healing and even empowermeant..

Bhagavad Gita Insight:
"Anger leads to delusion, delusion leads to confusion of memory; when memory is confused, intellect is lost; and when intellect is lost, one is ruined." — Chapter 2, Verse 63

4. Growth Through Bargaining: Moving from Desperation to Self-Reflection

Moving Beyond Bargaining

Bargaining is a natural response to loss, arising from an inherent desire to regain control of what feels uncontrollable. This reaction often appears as "what if's" and "if only's", in an attempt to change the past and undo the pain. While this phase is a normal part of healing, you will begin the process of re-authoring your new self when you recognize that it is time to move on and learn from the past, rather than trying to fix it.

The Process of Renewal

Be Present:
Mindful moments in life can aid in moving you to the here and now and pull you out of the infinite cycle of "what could have been."

Meditation helps you to feel fresh everytime you pass breathing therapy

Start living the little joys in your daily life to remind yourself that your healing is occurring in every moment.

Reflect and Learn:
Re-examine the relationship as a teacher.

What did the relationship teach you about yourself?

As you start your forward journey, recognize patterns or behaviors you want to change going forward. By reflecting, you are able to change your regret to growth.

ॐ

History will be rewritten no matter how hard you try, but you can leverage what you learned and create a better future.
By unlearning bargaining, you can let go of that death grip of what if, and take ownership of the here and now, intentionally. When you acknowledge what you have learned, you permit yourself to move forward with confidence, while creating separation from the past.

Self-Help Perspective:

"The only way to make sense out of change is to plunge into it, move with it, and join the dance." — Alan Watts

This over her is chatgpt generated

5. Growth Through Acceptance: Embracing Reality with Grace

The Stage of Acceptance

Acceptance does not mean you are okay with what transpired; it is simply accepting that reality and deciding to be okay to live with it. Accepting is when you stop

combating life and start relinquishing the resistance and move into acceptance. This is when growth starts—when you have no resistance to the inevitable, and you have made a little room for healing to take place, new possibilities to arise.

The Stage of Rebuilding
Envision your future:
Through acceptance, you create space for beginnings. This begins by creating a vision for a future that does not have the distinction of the pain of the past attached to it.

Set small steps to build upon this vision.
Cherish all of the little victories when you discover them because they are all evidence of your resilient capacity to withstand.

Focus on the process not the journey, not the perfection.
Recovery will be anything other than linear and it is acceptable to falter every now and then, just keep on moving. Every day you choose to give life a chance for what it is, you are becoming more resilient and prepared for what comes next.

ॐ

Acceptance is not the destination - it's the departure point. A shift from resistance to peace, from pain to possibility.

When you adopt acceptance as a doorway to freedom, that's what you will discover: opportunities for growth and change. In that place of surrender, you find the capacity to generate a life defined by who you are rather than by what has happened to you.

<u>Bhagavad Gita Wisdom:</u>
"A person is said to be established in self-realization when he

is fully satisfied in the self, by the self, with the self." —
Chapter 2, Verse 55

6. Growth Through Renewal: Rebuilding and Rediscovering Yourself

Renewal is the beautiful end of everything heartbreak taught you; when you realize that pain doesn't define you, but rather the person you became in spite of it. Renewal is when you push into a new chapter of your life with purpose, understanding, and strength..

Rediscover Passions:

Revisit some of your old hobbies or interests that you had been neglecting. Even though you haven't danced, painted, tended to your garden, or read a book in years, they still bring the pleasure and the value of life.

Cultivate Gratitude:

Concentrate your thinking on everything positive in your life. Think about the strength you have built and the development you have experienced. Remember, gratitude changes your manner of thinking and gives you hope and peace.

Form New Connections:

Surround yourself with people who can inspire you and encourage in growth. These connections can bring fresh energy and perspectives into your life.

Invest in Your Future:

Start learn new skills, or explore new places. Investing in yourself helps you in growing and starting of a new chapter

Renewal begins when you stop watching yourself as broken and start identify the strength and wisdom you've gained through challenges.

Quote from Literature:
"It's only after we've lost everything that we're free to do

anything." — Chuck Palahniuk, Fight Club
The Road Ahead

Growing and renewing after heartbreak doesn't mean going back to who you were; it is taking on a version of you that is wiser, stronger, and more aligned to your values. Each stage of this journey has its lessons, and each lesson brings deeper understanding: of your life, of love, of yourself.

<u>As the Bhagavad Gita teaches</u>:
"One who sees inaction in action, and action in inaction, is intelligent among men. Such a person is a yogi and is in the transcendental position." — Chapter 4, Verse 18

"In renewal, you find not just healing, but transformation. The pain was not in vain—it was the soil in which your new self grew."

Although the process of breaking up is intimate and personal, many may similarly consider how to enhance the process and stages of recovery more than just the beginning. These enhancements to the breakup process and its stages aim to create more clarity, resiliency, and meaning as you rebuild your life.

7. Growth Through Forgiveness: Releasing the Chains of the Past

Forgiveness does not mean freeing one from the pain, or excusing the pain that was inflicted on someone. Forgiveness is simply letting go of feelings of resentment or allowing one to move on.

The Action of Forgiveness

Forgive Yourself First: Be aware of any contribution you may have made but do not take ownership of someone else's actions. Growth is about the learning, not the destination.

Acknowledge Their Humanity: Understand that everyone started off different, with a different level of understanding and different experiences. This can help diminish feelings of anger and resentment.

Write a Forgiveness Letter and writing your feelings out by hand, even if you do not send it, can provide closure and a release of your feelings.

To hold on to those feelings of resentment, is to stay stuck in the past. Forgiveness gives you back your peace and gives you the opportunity to start fresh.

"*Quote from the Bhagavad Gita:*
"The wise should forgive all injuries and never harbor resentment." — Chapter 16, Verse 3"

8. Growth Through Gratitude: Focusing on Abundance
The Practice of Gratitude

Gratitude journal: Write down the things you are grateful for each day, no matter how small they may seem, they'll have a huge impact in the process

Celebrate the little wins: Even if no one else can share in your small accomplishments, you can! Healing is made by little wins. celebrate smallest achivements you've made.

Shift your viewpoint: Consider everything heartbreak has taught you, and how those lessons have made you stronger.

Gratitude rewires the brain so it can help with emotional resilience will diminish stress, and remind you where you find beauty and hope in your life, even in times of pain.

"
Quote from Literature:
"Gratitude unlocks the fullness of life. It turns what we have into enough, and more." — Melody Beattie
"

9. Personal Growth through Self-Discovery: A New Identity

When it comes to heartbreak, sometimes one can lose parts of their identity especially if their identity was tied to the relationship. Now, you can completely re-invent yourself.

The Art of Self-Discovery

Reconnect with Old Interests: Go back to some of your past hobbies or interests that you might have stopped reconsidering.

Explore New things: Get away from your comfort zone to experience new experiences, people, or activities.

Take some time to identify your values in order to be importance and live your life by them.

Heartbreak creates space for you to start fresh, to rebuild life on your own terms.

"This is your moment—be the real you."

"Quote from Literature:
"And now, let us welcome the new year, full of things that have never been." — Rainer Maria Rilke
"

10. Growth Through Service: Finding Purpose Beyond Yourself

Moving your attention beyond yourself can be incredibly healing. Helping other people leads you to meaning and perspective; your pain is not the end, but a pathway to greater compassion.

The Practice of Serving

Volunteer in Your Community: serve to the welfare of other people, in a shelter, at a government school, or a orphan age home can be incredibly satisfying.

Be a mentor: Express about your journey with someone else in similar situations.

Create for a Cause: Use your talent as a writer, artist, musician, etc. to raise awareness for the issues that matter to you or matters to the world.

Service reminds you that life exists outside of your pain. It uses your heartbreak as a foundation to inspire and connect you with yourself and others.

"Quote from Literature:
"The best way to find yourself is to lose yourself in the service of others." — Mahatma Gandhi"

11. Growth Through Mindfulness: Living Fully in the Present

Mindfulness is the state of being present without judgement or distraction. Mindfull is helpful in order to reduce emotional chaos

The Skills of Mindfulness

Meditation: In the morning or evening every day sit in silence and focus on your breath, *30 minutes everysingle day.*

Mindful Activities: Cook, walk, paint or do something with full attention.

Mindfulness allows us to detach from the stories or delusion we create about the past or the future, and keeps us stabled in the present where healing can occur.

Quote from the Bhagavad Gita:
"One who is controlled in mind, who has inner peace, and who remains balanced in joy and sorrow, success and failure, is truly a yogi." — Chapter 6, Verse 7

12. Growth Through Hope: Creating a Vision for the Future

Hope is light that shines through the dark night of heartbreak. It is faith that, perhaps not today, but tomorrow, better times are ahead of you, regardless of everything you've gone through.

A Hope Practice

Develop New Goals: Focus on the things that excite or inspire you, no matter how large or even small but future focused.

Envision Your Future: live the life you want to create yourself and start working on the position you've dreamed of.

Find Positive Settings: Listen to people, read books, create experiences that elevate you and encourage you to keep going and moving into the right direction.

Hope is what has you be strong within yourself and Hope is that light heat shines you forward, always reminding you, your best days are still yet to come.

> "*Quote from Literature:*
> "*Hope is the thing with feathers that perches in the soul, and sings the tune without the words, and never stops at all.*" — *Emily Dickinson*"

The Ongoing Cycle of Growth

Healing from heartbreak it's like reaching the final destination but about embracing the journey that taught you. Each step, no matter how small or big will make you closer to the growth

As you navigate this process, you should realize that heartbreak is never the end of an experience. It's the beginning of a metamorphosis that will evolve you into someone who embodies more wisdom, courage, and intellect, which will ultimately help you become more in line with your most authentic self.

"*In the words of the Bhagavad Gita:*
"No effort is ever wasted, and there is no failure."
— Chapter 2, Verse 40
Your journey of growth and renewal is a testament to your resilience. Embrace it fully, and you will emerge stronger than ever."

VII
THE ENTIRE STORY

Many of you may not fully grasp what was meant, so let me share a story—a journey through hurt, healing, and growth. It will explore how relationships begin, how they can cause pain, and how people find their way to healing. By the end, I'll answer the question: Are human relationships truly important to us?

lets start with falling in relationship through a story

As I sat down to tell my readers about the science behind love I thought, This should be a piece of cake. A splash of dopamine , a sprinkle of oxytocin, and a dash of serotonin to give it that spicy obsession touch. I couldn't have been more mistaken.

I started, "Love begins with dopamine—a chemical that makes you feel euphoric, like when you find fries at the bottom of the bag."

My friend interrupted, "So you're saying love is... like fast food?"

"No," I sighed. "Dopamine will makes you feel good around someone. It's like your brain is going, 'Wow, let's see them again, let us talk with them again, and again, and AGAIN.'"

"And oxytocin?" they asked.

"Ah, oxytocin is the 'cuddle hormone.' It's released during hugs, kisses, and, well, more-than-hugs. It's why you feel closer after a warm embrace. Basically, it's the glue."

They smirked. "So that's why people with commitment issues avoid hugs? Too much glue?"

"Exactly!" I grinned. "And let's not forget serotonin. It drops when you're falling for someone, making you obsess over them. Ever found yourself staring at your phone, waiting for a text? That's low serotonin, my friend. Your brain's like, This person is my entire Wi-Fi signal."

They laughed. "Okay, but why do we fall for specific people? What's the secret sauce?"

"Two words: symmetry and pheromones. Symmetry means their face is naturally pleasing to your brain, and pheromones are these invisible signals that scream, 'Hey, we'd make good-looking babies!'"

Their face lit up. "So love is basically chemistry class with extra credit in genetics?"

"Pretty much," I admitted. "Oh, and don't forget proximity. Spending time together boosts attraction. It's why people fall for classmates, coworkers, or even that neighbor who waters their plants like they're auditioning for a gardening reality show."

They leaned in, clearly enjoying this. "But what about reciprocity? Isn't that important?"

"Yes!" I exclaimed. "When someone likes you, your brain's like, Wait, they like me? Well, maybe I like them too! And boom, the cycle begins."

"So you're saying love is just a cocktail of chemicals and convenience?" they teased.

"Not just that," I corrected. "It's also shared values, experiences, and emotional connection. But the chemicals definitely keep things interesting. Love's like baking—a little science, a little art, and a whole lot of heartburn."

They burst out laughing. "I'll never look at love—or fries—the same way again."

ൠ

HURT

After my little talk about love (yeah, I might've sounded like a professor there), someone cut in:

"Okay, Professor Cupid, but what about when it all blows up? Like... breakups? What's going on in the brain then?"

I laughed. "Ah, breakups—the plot twist nobody wants. Think of it like uninstalling the most addictive app on your phone."

They raised an eyebrow. "Uninstalling? That sounds too easy."

"Oh, trust me, it's not." I shook my head. "First, your brain freaks out. Where's my dopamine? Where's my serotonin? It's like your brain is throwing a tantrum because the app that gave it daily happiness is gone."

"And then?" they pressed.

"Then the notifications start—memories. Your brain's like, Remember that smile in the rain? Remember that song you both loved? Basically, it keeps hitting replay at the worst possible times."

They groaned. "Ugh, the brain's greatest-hits album of pain."

"Exactly," I said, laughing. "It's not trying to torture you—it's just confused. Love wires your brain for connection. Breakups rip those wires out. Dopamine crashes, oxytocin disappears, and cortisol—the stress hormone—moves in like an unwanted roommate."

Their eyes went wide. "So that's why I felt like I was literally dying last time?"

"Pretty much," I nodded. "Heartbreak lights up the same brain areas as physical pain. That's why it feels like someone punched you in the chest. Your brain's screaming,

Danger! Fix this!"

They hesitated, then half-laughed. "And the crying?"

"Crying's just your body dumping stress," I explained. "Cortisol piles up, and tears are like the drain valve. It's your body saying, okay, okay, let's release some of this mess."

"Alright," they said, chuckling, "but what about that rage phase? The 'how dare they' mood?"

"That's your amygdala talking—the part that handles emotions like anger and betrayal. Meanwhile, your prefrontal cortex—the rational bit—is whispering in the background, please don't send that 2 AM text."

They smirked. "Let me guess—the amygdala usually wins?"

"Most of the time," I admitted, laughing. "But eventually, the storm passes. Your brain starts making happy chemicals again—from new sources. Friends, hobbies, even, uh... comfort food. Lots of it."

They leaned closer. "Okay, but what about that phase where you stalk your ex's Instagram at 3 AM?"

"Oh, classic," I sighed. "That's your brain hunting for closure. What went wrong? Are they happier without me? But honestly, it's a trap. The more you look, the more those wires stay tangled. It makes moving on way harder."

"Guilty," they muttered. "So when does the healing part actually start?"

"Healing's basically rewiring," I said. "You cut off contact, stop the late-night stalking, and start focusing on yourself. Slowly, your brain builds new pathways—from laughter with friends, new passions, even just small wins."

Their voice softened. "And the hurt? When does that stop?"

"It doesn't vanish overnight," I said. "But it shifts. Every tear, every sleepless night—that's your brain processing.

And one day you wake up a little lighter, a little stronger. You carry those lessons forward."

They leaned back. "So love lights the fire, but the breakup... teaches you how to rebuild?"

"Exactly," I smiled. "Breakups hurt, but they also teach, heal, and make you tougher. It's your brain's messy way of preparing you for something better."

They grinned. "And the next time I cry into a tub of ice cream?"

"Just remember," I said, "you're not just crying—you're rewiring."

☙

GROWTH

After I wrapped up my little lecture on love, someone blurted out,

"Alright, Professor Cupid... but what about growth? Do people really grow after all this mess? Or is that just something people say to sound wise?"

I laughed. "Fair question. Growth does happen. Let me throw a few names at you."

"Take Hardik Pandya. That guy's been through the wringer. Remember that interview fiasco? Suspended, trolled, humiliated—it must've been hell. Most people would've gone quiet. But Hardik? He rebuilt. Trained harder, focused only on cricket, came back stronger. Won a trophy with Gujarat Titans, then led India in T20s. He literally used the hate as fuel."

My friend leaned in. "So heartbreak doesn't always kill you?"

"Exactly. Sometimes it's the reset button."

"Mary Kom's story kills me every time," I continued. "She went through something no parent should—losing her first child to a miscarriage. That pain could've finished her. But instead, she turned it into drive. Six-time world champion. That's not just sports—that's grit."

"Wow," they whispered. "That's heavy... but inspiring."

"And Sushant Singh Rajput," I said softly. "He had doors slammed in his face again and again. Rejections, gossip about his personal life—it was rough. But did he stop? No. He poured himself into learning. Physics, coding, music—you name it, he tried it. Every 'no' pushed him to expand himself."

They nodded quietly.

"And Oprah," I added. "Trauma, heartbreak, all of it. But instead of staying broken, she built herself into a global icon. That's self-growth on another level."

"Okay, but how does growth actually happen?" my friend asked.

"It's a mix," I said. "You reflect on yourself—what you really want, where you went wrong. Pain toughens you. You chase goals you were putting off. And you learn empathy—you start seeing other people's pain differently."

"And honestly," I added, "this isn't just about celebrities. Think about your own life. That failure in college you thought you'd never recover from? Or that breakup you thought would crush you? You came out of those stronger, didn't you?"

They smiled. "Yeah. Hurt like hell, but I did."

"Exactly," I said. "Growth is like the gym. It hurts, but the pain shapes you."

They laughed. "So heartbreak is like emotional workout class?"

"Pretty much," I grinned. "Pain's the workout, healing is the cool-down, and growth is when you see the changes in the mirror. Worth it, right?"

VIII

HOW TO BE SELF SATISFIED

The thing about happiness is—it's slippery. You run after it, the way a dog spins around trying to catch its own tail. And let me tell you, you probably won't grab it the way you imagine. But that's fine. The chase itself can still be worth something.

For years, I thought happiness was tied to upgrades. A new iPhone. A wardrobe refresh. People dropping "you look amazing" under my photos. And sure, it gave me a boost for a little while. But the shine faded quickly. That's when it struck me—happiness was never in the stuff, or in faster Wi-Fi. It was in the little things I barely noticed. Moments of gratitude. Quiet, simple things that had been there all along.

Here's my daily routine:

Step 1: Wake up.

Step 2: Realize I'm alive.

Step 3: Have coffee.

Step 4: Find joy in the fact that my coffee is not cold yet. (Trust me, that's a win.)

One day I tried this thing people talk about—writing down three things I was grateful for. Honestly, it felt like a joke. Three things? I could barely think of one. But I forced myself. And weirdly enough, it started working.

Like—hey, I didn't step on a Lego this morning. That's a win.

Or that sweet relief when you finally find your phone after ten minutes of searching and it's... in your pocket.

Or realizing you don't have a meeting for another whole hour.

Sounds trivial, right? Because it is. But those tiny things? They add up. Gratitude is like duct tape—it somehow fixes everything, even when you're falling apart.

I used to believe happiness was about more. More money, more status, more followers. But honestly? It's like cake. You eat a giant slice and then want another, and another, and no matter how much you eat, you never feel full. That's what chasing "more" feels like—endless, unsatisfying.

My friend Ravi is proof. He landed a big promotion, and we all thought he'd made it. Six months later, he called me up: "I hate my job. I don't even have time for lunch anymore. What's the point?"

I told him straight: "Bro, you traded peace of mind for a pay raise. Worth it?"

Spoiler: he quit. No backup plan, no grand vision. Just the realization that "more" wasn't giving him happiness.

The truth? Happiness isn't about piling things on. It's about noticing what's already there. Even if it's as silly as guilt-free binge-watching a whole season of Friends.

And then there's self-satisfaction. That's the real secret. And it doesn't come from a new car or fancy shoes (unless they're insanely comfortable, in which case, fine). Self-satisfaction is knowing you did your best—even if today your "best" was just getting out of bed, putting on pants, and not crying in the supermarket aisle.

I realized I was spending all my energy chasing opportunities but barely investing in the things that actually mattered to me—family, friends, food (mostly food, let's be honest). My relationships were slipping, and my free time was disappearing faster than my cooking experiments.

So I made a few changes. No more endless scrolling before bed. No more skipping lunch for "just one more task." Instead, I started showing up where it counted.

Playing video games with my brother—because honestly, that's the only therapy I trust.

Actually listening when someone talks, instead of just nodding while planning my next snack.

And yeah, spending proper time with my couch. Because sometimes, the couch really is the best company.

One day I tried this thing people keep talking about—writing down three things I was grateful for. Honestly, I thought it was a joke. Three things? I could barely think of one. But fine, I gave it a shot.

First thought: hey, I didn't step on a Lego this morning. That counts.

Second: that sweet relief when you finally find your phone after searching for ten minutes... and yeah, it was under the pillow the whole time.

Third: realizing I didn't have a meeting for another hour. Felt like winning the lottery.

They sound silly, right? Because they are.

But those little things matter. Gratitude is kind of like duct tape - it won't make your life perfect - but it somehow holds everything together when you are falling apart.

For a long time, I thought happiness meant more. More money, more status, more followers. Similar to cake; you have a big slice and then you want another, and another, no matter how much cake you consume you never feel satiated. That is how pursuing "more" feels - endless and unpleasurable.

Take my friend Ravi. He got a big promotion, and we were all like, "He's made it!" Six months later, he calls me: "I hate my job. I don't even get time for lunch anymore. What's the point?"

And I told him, "Bro, you literally traded peace of mind for a pay raise. Was it worth it?"

Spoiler: he quit. No plan, nothing lined up. Just realized that more money didn't mean more happiness.

Here's the thing—happiness isn't about stacking more and more. It's about actually noticing what you already have. Even if it's just guilt-free binge-watching a whole season of Friends. That's still happiness.

Now self-satisfaction? That's the real deal. And it doesn't come from cars or brands (unless the shoes are ridiculously comfy). It comes from knowing you showed up, even if today "showing up" meant dragging yourself out of bed, putting on pants, and not crying in the supermarket.

I started asking myself what actually mattered. Family. Friends. Food (yeah, mostly food). And I realized I was so busy chasing everything else that I wasn't giving these enough time. My relationships were slipping. My personal time? Gone.

So I made some rules. No scrolling before bed. No skipping lunch for "just one more task." Instead, I started showing up where it counts:

Playing video games with my brother—because honestly, that's therapy.

Actually listening when someone talks instead of nodding while thinking about my next snack.

And giving proper time to my couch. Because sometimes the couch is exactly what you need.

ဢ

Here's is the philosophy of the AYAN RAND
Embrace the Power Within You

The journey to self-growth begins with one truth: you are the architect of your own life. It begins with recognizing you are not your past, you are not your failures, you are not other people's opinions. You are what you choose to be today and what you will do moving forward. The road to self-growth is not always easy, but the effort is always worthwhile.

To begin self-growth, accept yourself totally, strengths and weaknesses, flaws and virtues alike. Self-acceptance is not an excuse to do nothing, rather it is allowing yourself the space to grow, make mistakes, and get up again with even more wisdom. You can then become who you are

Next, it's time to take ownership of your life. It's easy to blame other people, circumstances, or the world for your problems. However, true personal growth happens when you realize you are capable of changing your circumstances. Your choices now will define your future. By taking ownership, you are also taking control and empowering yourself to take action.

Set intentions around where you want to obtain. Clarity is essential. Know what you want and focus your energy into getting there. Break down your larger intentions into smaller steps, and adjust as necessary. Understand that change doesn't happen in one straight line. Change is a process. It's ok to take wrong turns along the way, or take breaks. What's important is to keep moving forward.

And, lastly, time & persistence is key. Growth takes time; it is not a race. There will be days when doubt arises, setbacks occur, and frustration takes over; each time an obstacle arises is another learning opportunity.

"The man who thinks must think and act his own the reasoning mind cannot work under any form of complusion, it cannot be subordinated to the needs, opinion or wishes of others, it is not an object of sacrifice "

DOES RELATIONSHIP MATTERS?

Whether relationships are beneficial is somewhat dependent on the individual. For someone feeling vulnerable or uncertain, a partner can greatly help someone get back on their feet. Others might feel relationships are not essential, especially those with an endless number of dreams or ambitions, and those see relationships as optional aspects to their lives, only something they think about if it helps attain their goals.

In society, we are often judged or molded externally (our beliefs or even outward appearance) to certain expectations of behavior. If someone discourages a particular behavior or journey, whether that's following a dream, pursuing a passion, or finding individuality, those discouragements seem to come not just from society but at times from those rather close to you. Friends may discourage you out of kindness, concern, or fear of failing but they also likely don't see a clear path for you; thus unintentionally stunting your growth. Worst yet, an unsupportive partner likely has the potential to do all of the above.

A partner will help you to shows your strengths, even if you cannot see them yourself. A partner can support you to see your own greatness and give you momentum to pursue your meaningful career or bold goals. Consider a student weighed down by schoolwork and other life issues. For some, relationships become a distraction. However, a truly supportive relationship can become a life raft. It can encourage and focus your efforts to sustain you through obstacles.

For example:

A student working to get ready for a challenging exam with very little chance for success, who has gotten rejected over and over, may feel defeated. Simply knowing that someone is in their corner is helpful; they are encouraged, motivated to focus on what mattered to them, and moving forward to achieve their goals.

Many entrepreneurs, like for example, Sara Blakely the founder of Spanx, refer to a supportive environment

On the other hand, many people treat relationships as simply a means to while away the hours and not as a meaningful connection at all, which I think is especially common among students who are often not fully comprehending that you can enjoy and get a lot from a relationship, when it is built on mutual growth and encouragement.

In fact, there are plenty of success stories showing that having a great support system - a partner, friend, or mentor - can help turn a negative into a positive. A healthy relationship provides more than just emotional support; it can be a catalyst for growth, and tends to motivate people to do better and grow.

MY WORDS

Romantic relationships? No thanks, I'm not interested. I mean honestly, who in their right mind jumps on an emotional rollercoaster that might torch with sleepless nights? Who would want to let themselves be broken by someone like a cheap coffee mug?Not me. Nope. Thank you, heart and heart.

And don't even get me started on breakups. Crying for six straight hours? Ben and Jerry's pints while I mourn my insignificant love life that I've allowed to totlly consume my existence while re-watching a sad movie? Nope. To me, it makes much more sense to put my head down, sleep peacefully, unbothered, and dream about a life that doesn't have me waiting around for someone else's text reply. You can't "leave me on read" when I'm single, right?

To be frankly honest, I'm not even getting whole conversations with my best friend. I'm a bad friend to her and she's pretty upset with me (which is fair!). OMG Dude, if you're reading this, un-block me. I swear I will make it up to you!

How can I think about living in a relationship line when I can't even manage to keep my friendships amicable?

So yes, I will be happy as a single person please! No late-night arguments, thank you!

I'll stay single, cook my own biryani, enjoy my own company—flirt with myself, and even cry over my own food. Biryani is the hottest thing I'll ever own. And honestly, you should try it too.

Provide an honest rating for this book on both Amazon and Flipkart.

৪৩

"Thank you for taking the time to read this book. I truly hope it brings you happiness and helps guide you toward a beautiful life.

Feel free to reach out to me anytime via Instagram. As a mental health advocate and emotional supporter, I'm always here to lend a helping hand."

PALLE VASU

Palle Vasu, a 21-year-old author and former forest department employee, discovered his passion for writing while exploring the beauty of nature. Now fully dedicated to building a career as a writer, he uses his experiences and insights to craft stories that inspire and connect with readers, sharing his unique journey through the pages of his books.

Instagram; @palle_vasu
Mail: vasusign2580@gmail.com

www.ingramcontent.com/pod-product-compliance
Lightning Source LLC
Chambersburg PA
CBHW061434160726
47995CB00003B/894